Thoughts At F___It Forties

Gilda Tavernese

Thoughts At F__It Forties
Copyright © 2022 by Gilda Tavernese

Tellwell Talent
www.tellwell.ca

ISBN
978-0-2288-7787-5 (Hardcover)
978-0-2288-7786-8 (Paperback)

"Welcome to the beginning! It's truly the best place to start. I sometimes find gratitude journals intimidating because like most of you, I am not always able to see the bright side of my day. Some days I just want to scream and vent, and often obsess about how awful an experience has been. I hope this journal can help you capture not only all the wonderful things that you are grateful for, or the fabulous things that have happened to you daily–but feel free to also write down what has angered you or is bugging you. It can be just as cathartic as jotting down all your positive thoughts.

Of course, what I hope for you is that your left column will always be longer than your right one!

Take your time and go easy on yourself. Don't forget, there is no wrong way to do this gratitude journal thing....the hardest part is starting and you have already begun!"

Gilda
XOX

Stay in touch!
Let me know how your journaling is going

gilda.tavernese@gmail.com

Follow me on social media under TAFF.blog

Gilda Tavernese is a writer, blogger, and former psychotherapist with a Master of Social Work from the University of Toronto. She resides in Canada with her two children and her beloved teacup poodle, Luna..., and of course her husband!

Thoughts At F___It Forties

Thoughts That Make Me Smile: F___It Thoughts:

- _____
- _____
- _____
- _____
- _____
- _____
- _____

_____

_____

"I wish you happy thoughts,
and manageable heavy ones too!"

(Blog: Funny Thoughts After 40!
Author: Gilda Tavernese)

Thoughts At F___It Forties

Thoughts That Make Me Smile: F__It Thoughts:

- _____
- _____
- _____
- _____
- _____
- _____
- _____

_____

_____

_____

_____

_____

Thoughts At F___It Forties

Thoughts That Make Me Smile: F___It Thoughts:

- _____

- _____

- _____

- _____

- _____

- _____

_____

_____

_____

_____

Thoughts At F___It Forties

Thoughts That Make Me Smile: F___It Thoughts:

* _____

* _____

* _____

* _____

* _____

* _____

* _____

_____

_____

_____

_____

_____

Thoughts At F___It Forties

Thoughts That Make Me Smile: F__It Thoughts:

- _____

- _____

- _____

- _____

- _____

- _____

- _____

_____

_____

_____

_____

_____

Thoughts At F___It Forties

Thoughts That Make Me Smile: F___It Thoughts:

- _____
- _____
- _____
- _____
- _____
- _____
- _____

_____

_____

_____

_____

Date: _____

Thoughts At F___It Forties

Thoughts That Make Me Smile: F___It Thoughts:

- _____
- _____
- _____
- _____
- _____
- _____
- _____

_____

_____

_____

_____

Date: _____

Thoughts At F___It Forties

Thoughts That Make Me Smile: **F___It Thoughts:**

- _____

- _____

- _____

- _____

- _____

- _____

- _____

_____

_____

_____

_____

8

Thoughts At F___It Forties

Thoughts That Make Me Smile: F___It Thoughts:

- _____
- _____
- _____
- _____
- _____
- _____
- _____

_____

_____

_____

_____

_____

Thoughts At F___It Forties

Thoughts That Make Me Smile: F___It Thoughts:

- _____
- _____
- _____
- _____
- _____
- _____
- _____

_____

_____

*"I think I've grown out of the need to
be liked by everyone in this world."*

*(Blog: Sticking Your Neck Out, Is it Worth It?
Author: Gilda Tavernese)*

Thoughts At F___It Forties

Thoughts That Make Me Smile: F___It Thoughts:

- _____
- _____
- _____
- _____
- _____
- _____
- _____

_____

_____

_____

_____

Date: _____

Thoughts At F___It Forties

Thoughts That Make Me Smile: F___It Thoughts:

- _____

- _____

- _____

- _____

- _____

- _____

- _____

_____

_____

_____

_____

Thoughts At F___It Forties

Thoughts That Make Me Smile: F___It Thoughts:

- _____

- _____

- _____

- _____

- _____

- _____

- _____

_____

_____

_____

_____

_____

Thoughts At F___It Forties

Thoughts That Make Me Smile: F___It Thoughts:

- _____
- _____
- _____
- _____
- _____
- _____
- _____

_____

_____

_____

_____

_____

Thoughts At F___It Forties

Thoughts That Make Me Smile: F___It Thoughts:

- _____
- _____
- _____
- _____
- _____
- _____
- _____

_____

_____

_____

_____

Thoughts At F___It Forties

Thoughts That Make Me Smile: F___It Thoughts:

- _____
- _____
- _____
- _____
- _____
- _____
- _____

_____

_____

_____

_____

Thoughts At F___It Forties

Thoughts That Make Me Smile: **F___It Thoughts:**

- _____
- _____
- _____
- _____
- _____
- _____
- _____

_____

_____

_____

_____

_____

Thoughts At F___It Forties

Thoughts That Make Me Smile: F___It Thoughts:

- _____

- _____

- _____

- _____

- _____

- _____

- _____

_____

_____

"I have learned not to hide from it, to verbalize it, to name it and to normalize it."

(Blog: Not Just The Jitters
Author: Gilda Tavernese)

Thoughts At F___It Forties

Thoughts That Make Me Smile: F___It Thoughts:

- _____
- _____
- _____
- _____
- _____
- _____
- _____

_____

_____

_____

_____

Thoughts At F___It Forties

Thoughts That Make Me Smile: F___It Thoughts:

- _____

- _____

- _____

- _____

- _____

- _____

- _____

_____

_____

_____

_____

Thoughts At F___It Forties

Thoughts That Make Me Smile: **F___It Thoughts:**

- _____

- _____

- _____

- _____

- _____

- _____

_____

_____

_____

_____

_____

Date: _____

Thoughts At F___It Forties

Thoughts That Make Me Smile: F___It Thoughts:

- _____

- _____

- _____

- _____

- _____

- _____

- _____

_____

_____

_____

_____

Thoughts At F___It Forties

Thoughts That Make Me Smile: F___It Thoughts:

- _____

- _____

- _____

- _____

- _____

- _____

- _____

_____

_____

_____

_____

Thoughts At F___It Forties

Thoughts That Make Me Smile: F___It Thoughts:

- _____

- _____

- _____

- _____

- _____

- _____

- _____

_____

_____

_____

_____

Thoughts At F___It Forties

Thoughts That Make Me Smile: **F___It Thoughts:**

- _____

- _____

- _____

- _____

- _____

- _____

- _____

_____

_____

_____

_____

_____

Thoughts At F___It Forties

Thoughts That Make Me Smile: F___It Thoughts:

- _____

- _____

- _____

- _____

- _____

- _____

- _____

_____

_____

"I fell into the abyss of mourning. It was deep and wide and felt dark and endless."

*(Blog: Part 1: Coincidence? I Think Not
Author: Gilda Tavernese)*

Thoughts At F___It Forties

Thoughts That Make Me Smile: F___It Thoughts:

- _____
- _____
- _____
- _____
- _____
- _____
- _____

_____

_____

_____

_____

Date: _____

Thoughts At F___It Forties

Thoughts That Make Me Smile: F__It Thoughts:

-
-
-
-
-
-
-

Thoughts At F___It Forties

Thoughts That Make Me Smile: F__It Thoughts:

- _____

- _____

- _____

- _____

- _____

- _____

- _____

_____

_____

_____

_____

Thoughts At F___It Forties

Thoughts That Make Me Smile: **F__It Thoughts:**

- _____
- _____
- _____
- _____
- _____
- _____
- _____

_____

_____

_____

_____

Thoughts At F___It Forties

Thoughts That Make Me Smile: F___It Thoughts:

- _____

- _____

- _____

- _____

- _____

- _____

- _____

_____

_____

_____

_____

Thoughts At F___It Forties

Thoughts That Make Me Smile: F___It Thoughts:

- _____
- _____
- _____
- _____
- _____
- _____
- _____

_____

_____

_____

_____

_____

Thoughts At F___It Forties

Thoughts That Make Me Smile: F___It Thoughts:

- _____
- _____
- _____
- _____
- _____
- _____
- _____

_____

_____

_____

_____

Thoughts At F___It Forties

Thoughts That Make Me Smile: F__It Thoughts:

- _____
- _____
- _____
- _____
- _____
- _____
- _____

_____

_____

"I simply don't believe in coincidences.
Our actions have purpose.
Our thoughts have meaning."

(Blog: Part 2: Coincidence? I Think Not
Author: Gilda Tavernese)

Date: _____

Thoughts At F___It Forties

Thoughts That Make Me Smile: F___It Thoughts:

- _____
- _____
- _____
- _____
- _____
- _____
- _____

_____

_____

_____

_____

Thoughts At F___It Forties

Thoughts That Make Me Smile: F___It Thoughts:

- _____

- _____

- _____

- _____

- _____

- _____

- _____

_____

_____

_____

_____

Thoughts At F___It Forties

Thoughts That Make Me Smile: F___It Thoughts:

- _____
- _____
- _____
- _____
- _____
- _____
- _____

_____

_____

_____

_____

Thoughts At F___It Forties

Thoughts That Make Me Smile: F___It Thoughts:

* _____
* _____
* _____
* _____
* _____
* _____
* _____

_____

_____

_____

_____

Thoughts At F___It Forties

Thoughts That Make Me Smile: **F___It Thoughts:**

- _____
- _____
- _____
- _____
- _____
- _____
- _____

_____

_____

_____

_____

Thoughts At F___It Forties

Thoughts That Make Me Smile: F___It Thoughts:

- _____

- _____

- _____

- _____

- _____

- _____

- _____

_____

_____

_____

_____

Thoughts At F___It Forties

Thoughts That Make Me Smile: F___It Thoughts:

- _____
- _____
- _____
- _____
- _____
- _____
- _____

_____

_____

_____

_____

Thoughts At F___It Forties

Thoughts That Make Me Smile: F___It Thoughts:

- _____
- _____
- _____
- _____
- _____
- _____
- _____

_____

_____

"...Every time I say goodnight and squeeze her tight, she seems to have taken flight and grown overnight..."

(Blog: A Mother's Goodnight Blues
Author: Gilda Tavernese)

Thoughts At F___It Forties

Thoughts That Make Me Smile: F___It Thoughts:

- _____
- _____
- _____
- _____
- _____
- _____
- _____

_____

_____

_____

_____

Thoughts At F___It Forties

Thoughts That Make Me Smile: F__It Thoughts:

- _____

- _____

- _____

- _____

- _____

- _____

- _____

_____

_____

_____

_____

Thoughts At F___It Forties

Thoughts That Make Me Smile: F___It Thoughts:

- _____
- _____
- _____
- _____
- _____
- _____
- _____

_____

_____

_____

_____

Thoughts At F___It Forties

Thoughts That Make Me Smile: F__It Thoughts:

- _____

- _____

- _____

- _____

- _____

- _____

- _____

_____

_____

_____

_____

Thoughts At F___It Forties

Thoughts That Make Me Smile: F__It Thoughts:

- _____
- _____
- _____
- _____
- _____
- _____
- _____

_____

_____

_____

_____

Thoughts At F___It Forties

Thoughts That Make Me Smile: F___It Thoughts:

- _____

- _____

- _____

- _____

- _____

- _____

- _____

_____

_____

_____

_____

Thoughts At F___It Forties

Thoughts That Make Me Smile:　　　F___It Thoughts:

- _____
- _____
- _____
- _____
- _____
- _____
- _____

_____

_____

_____

_____

_____

Thoughts At F___It Forties

Thoughts That Make Me Smile: **F__It Thoughts:**

- _____

- _____

- _____

- _____

- _____

- _____

- _____

_____

_____

"I believe 'fancy' is a state of mind
that I often choose to be in."

(Blog: Stay Fancy!
Author: Gilda Tavernese)

Thoughts At F___It Forties

Thoughts That Make Me Smile: F___It Thoughts:

- _____
- _____
- _____
- _____
- _____
- _____
- _____

_____

_____

_____

_____

Thoughts At F___It Forties

Thoughts That Make Me Smile: **F___It Thoughts:**

- _____
- _____
- _____
- _____
- _____
- _____
- _____

_____

_____

_____

_____

Thoughts At F___It Forties

Thoughts That Make Me Smile: F___It Thoughts:

- _____
- _____
- _____
- _____
- _____
- _____
- _____

_____

_____

_____

_____

Thoughts At F___It Forties

Thoughts That Make Me Smile: F__It Thoughts:

- _____
- _____
- _____
- _____
- _____
- _____
- _____

_____

_____

_____

_____

Thoughts At F___It Forties

Thoughts That Make Me Smile: F___It Thoughts:

- _____
- _____
- _____
- _____
- _____
- _____
- _____

_____

_____

_____

_____

Thoughts At F___It Forties

Thoughts That Make Me Smile: F___It Thoughts:

- _____

- _____

- _____

- _____

- _____

- _____

- _____

_____

_____

_____

_____

Thoughts At F___It Forties

Thoughts That Make Me Smile: F___It Thoughts:

- _____
- _____
- _____
- _____
- _____
- _____
- _____

_____

_____

_____

_____

Date: _____

Thoughts At F___It Forties

Thoughts That Make Me Smile: F___It Thoughts:

- _____
- _____
- _____
- _____
- _____
- _____
- _____

_____

_____

"A genuine, authentic, forthright woman is always beautiful."

(Blog: Stay Fancy!
Author: Gilda Tavernese)

Thoughts At F___It Forties

Thoughts That Make Me Smile: **F___It Thoughts:**

- _____

- _____

- _____

- _____

- _____

- _____

- _____

_____

_____

_____

_____

Thoughts At F___It Forties

Thoughts That Make Me Smile: F___It Thoughts:

- _____
- _____
- _____
- _____
- _____
- _____
- _____

_____

_____

_____

_____

Thoughts At F___It Forties

Thoughts That Make Me Smile: F___It Thoughts:

- _____
- _____
- _____
- _____
- _____
- _____
- _____

_____

_____

_____

_____

Thoughts At F___It Forties

Thoughts That Make Me Smile: F___It Thoughts:

- _____

- _____

- _____

- _____

- _____

- _____

- _____

_____

_____

_____

_____

_____

Thoughts At F___It Forties

Thoughts That Make Me Smile: **F___It Thoughts:**

- _____

- _____

- _____

- _____

- _____

- _____

- _____

_____

_____

_____

_____

Thoughts At F___It Forties

Thoughts That Make Me Smile: F___It Thoughts:

- _____

- _____

- _____

- _____

- _____

- _____

- _____

_____

_____

_____

_____

Thoughts At F___It Forties

Thoughts That Make Me Smile: F___It Thoughts:

- _____

- _____

- _____

- _____

- _____

- _____

- _____

_____

_____

_____

_____

_____

Date: _____

Thoughts At F___It Forties

Thoughts That Make Me Smile: F___It Thoughts:

- _____
- _____
- _____
- _____
- _____
- _____
- _____

_____

"...after I've stabilized myself, I find the ore to paddle forward...strokes are short and weak, but nevertheless forward is my direction, in the end guided by my best compass–my intuition."

(Blog: How I Get Over A Brick Wall
Author: Gilda Tavernese)

66

Thoughts At F___It Forties

Thoughts That Make Me Smile: **F___It Thoughts:**

- _____

- _____

- _____

- _____

- _____

- _____

- _____

_____

_____

_____

_____

Thoughts At F___It Forties

Thoughts That Make Me Smile: F___It Thoughts:

- _____
- _____
- _____
- _____
- _____
- _____
- _____

_____

_____

_____

_____

Thoughts At F___It Forties

Thoughts That Make Me Smile: F___It Thoughts:

- _____

- _____

- _____

- _____

- _____

- _____

- _____

_____

_____

_____

_____

Thoughts At F___It Forties

Thoughts That Make Me Smile: F__It Thoughts:

- _____
- _____
- _____
- _____
- _____
- _____
- _____

_____

_____

_____

_____

Thoughts At F___It Forties

Thoughts That Make Me Smile: F___It Thoughts:

- _____
- _____
- _____
- _____
- _____
- _____
- _____

_____

_____

_____

_____

Thoughts At F___It Forties

Thoughts That Make Me Smile: **F__It Thoughts:**

- _____
- _____
- _____
- _____
- _____
- _____
- _____

_____

_____

_____

_____

Thoughts At F___It Forties

Thoughts That Make Me Smile:　　F___It Thoughts:

- _____
- _____
- _____
- _____
- _____
- _____
- _____

_____

_____

_____

_____

Date: _____

Thoughts At F___It Forties

Thoughts That Make Me Smile: F___It Thoughts:

- _____
- _____
- _____
- _____
- _____
- _____
- _____

_____

_____

"Perfectionists make the perfect procrastinators."

(Blog: Perfect Procrastinator
Author: Gilda Tavernese)

Date: _____

Thoughts At F___It Forties

Thoughts That Make Me Smile: F___It Thoughts:

- _____

- _____

- _____

- _____

- _____

- _____

- _____

_____

_____

_____

_____

75

Thoughts At F___It Forties

Thoughts That Make Me Smile: F__It Thoughts:

- _____

- _____

- _____

- _____

- _____

- _____

- _____

_____

_____

_____

_____

Thoughts At F___It Forties

Thoughts That Make Me Smile: F___It Thoughts:

- _____
- _____
- _____
- _____
- _____
- _____
- _____

_____

_____

_____

_____

Thoughts At F___It Forties

Thoughts That Make Me Smile: F___It Thoughts:

- _____
- _____
- _____
- _____
- _____
- _____
- _____

_____

_____

_____

_____

Date: _____

Thoughts At F___It Forties

Thoughts That Make Me Smile: F___It Thoughts:

- _____
- _____
- _____
- _____
- _____
- _____
- _____

_____

_____

_____

_____

Thoughts At F___It Forties

Thoughts That Make Me Smile: F__It Thoughts:

- _____
- _____
- _____
- _____
- _____
- _____
- _____

_____

_____

_____

_____

Thoughts At F___It Forties

Thoughts That Make Me Smile: **F___It Thoughts:**

- _____
- _____
- _____
- _____
- _____
- _____
- _____

_____

_____

_____

_____

Thoughts At F___It Forties

Thoughts That Make Me Smile: F___It Thoughts:

- _____
- _____
- _____
- _____
- _____
- _____
- _____

"Spoken words cannot be unspoken or taken back. They need only to be acknowledged. The words, along with the pain, need to be acknowledged before asking for forgiveness."

(Blog: The Art Of Forgiveness
Author: Gilda Tavernese)

Thoughts At F___It Forties

Thoughts That Make Me Smile: F___It Thoughts:

- _____
- _____
- _____
- _____
- _____
- _____
- _____

_____

_____

_____

_____

Thoughts At F___It Forties

Thoughts That Make Me Smile: F___It Thoughts:

- _____

- _____

- _____

- _____

- _____

- _____

- _____

_____

_____

_____

_____

Thoughts At F___It Forties

Thoughts That Make Me Smile: F___It Thoughts:

- _____

- _____

- _____

- _____

- _____

- _____

- _____

_____

_____

_____

_____

Thoughts At F___It Forties

Thoughts That Make Me Smile: F__It Thoughts:

- _____
- _____
- _____
- _____
- _____
- _____
- _____

_____

_____

_____

_____

Thoughts At F___It Forties

Thoughts That Make Me Smile: F__It Thoughts:

- _____
- _____
- _____
- _____
- _____
- _____
- _____

_____

_____

_____

_____

Thoughts At F___It Forties

Thoughts That Make Me Smile: F__It Thoughts:

- _____

- _____

- _____

- _____

- _____

- _____

- _____

_____

_____

_____

_____

Thoughts At F___It Forties

Thoughts That Make Me Smile: **F___It Thoughts:**

- _____
- _____
- _____
- _____
- _____
- _____
- _____

_____

_____

_____

_____

Thoughts At F___It Forties

Thoughts That Make Me Smile: F___It Thoughts:

- _____

- _____

- _____

- _____

- _____

- _____

- _____

_____

_____

*"Tell me, what could be better
than the melody of March?"*

*(Blog: The Melody Of March
Author: Gilda Tavernese)*

Thoughts At F___It Forties

Thoughts That Make Me Smile: F__It Thoughts:

- _____
- _____
- _____
- _____
- _____
- _____
- _____

_____

_____

_____

_____

Thoughts At F___It Forties

Thoughts That Make Me Smile: F___It Thoughts:

- _____
- _____
- _____
- _____
- _____
- _____
- _____

_____

_____

_____

_____

Thoughts At F___It Forties

Thoughts That Make Me Smile: **F___It Thoughts:**

- _____
- _____
- _____
- _____
- _____
- _____
- _____

_____

_____

_____

_____

Date: _____

Thoughts At F___It Forties

Thoughts That Make Me Smile: F___It Thoughts:

- _____

- _____

- _____

- _____

- _____

- _____

- _____

_____

_____

_____

_____

Thoughts At F___It Forties

Thoughts That Make Me Smile: F__It Thoughts:

- _____
- _____
- _____
- _____
- _____
- _____
- _____

_____

_____

_____

_____

Thoughts At F___It Forties

Thoughts That Make Me Smile: F___It Thoughts:

- _____
- _____
- _____
- _____
- _____
- _____
- _____

_____

_____

_____

_____

Thoughts At F___It Forties

Thoughts That Make Me Smile: F__It Thoughts:

- _____

- _____

- _____

- _____

- _____

- _____

- _____

_____

_____

_____

_____

Thoughts At F___It Forties

Thoughts That Make Me Smile: F___It Thoughts:

- _____
- _____
- _____
- _____
- _____
- _____
- _____

_____

_____

"I will forever be their number one fan,
as well as their greatest critic."

(Blog: I May Lay Them Down To Sleep…
But They Are Not Mine To Keep
Author: Gilda Tavernese)

Thoughts At F___It Forties

Thoughts That Make Me Smile: **F__It Thoughts:**

- _____
- _____
- _____
- _____
- _____
- _____
- _____

_____

_____

_____

_____

Thoughts At F___It Forties

Thoughts That Make Me Smile: F___It Thoughts:

- _____
- _____
- _____
- _____
- _____
- _____
- _____

_____

_____

_____

_____

Thoughts At F___It Forties

Thoughts That Make Me Smile: **F___It Thoughts:**

- _____

- _____

- _____

- _____

- _____

- _____

- _____

_____

_____

_____

_____

Thoughts At F___It Forties

Thoughts That Make Me Smile: F__It Thoughts:

- _____

- _____

- _____

- _____

- _____

- _____

- _____

_____

_____

_____

_____

Thoughts At F___It Forties

Thoughts That Make Me Smile: F__It Thoughts:

- _____
- _____
- _____
- _____
- _____
- _____
- _____

_____

_____

_____

_____

Date: _____

Thoughts At F___It Forties

Thoughts That Make Me Smile: F__It Thoughts:

- _____
- _____
- _____
- _____
- _____
- _____
- _____

_____
_____
_____
_____

Date: _____

Thoughts At F___It Forties

Thoughts That Make Me Smile: F___It Thoughts:

- _____
- _____
- _____
- _____
- _____
- _____
- _____

_____

_____

_____

_____

Date: _____

Thoughts At F___It Forties

Thoughts That Make Me Smile: F__It Thoughts:

- _____
- _____
- _____
- _____
- _____
- _____
- _____

_____

"Hey! I think it's time to do something very important-absolutely nothing at all for an extended period of time-to see where our mind takes us..."

(Blog: The Bad Word...Bored!
Author: Gilda Tavernese)

Thoughts At F___It Forties

Thoughts That Make Me Smile: F___It Thoughts:

- _____
- _____
- _____
- _____
- _____
- _____
- _____

_____

_____

_____

_____

Thoughts At F___It Forties

Thoughts That Make Me Smile: F__It Thoughts:

- _____

- _____

- _____

- _____

- _____

- _____

- _____

_____

_____

_____

_____

Thoughts At F___It Forties

Thoughts That Make Me Smile: F__It Thoughts:

- _____
- _____
- _____
- _____
- _____
- _____
- _____

_____

_____

_____

_____

_____

Thoughts At F___It Forties

Thoughts That Make Me Smile: F__It Thoughts:

- _____
- _____
- _____
- _____
- _____
- _____
- _____

_____

_____

_____

_____

Thoughts At F___It Forties

Thoughts That Make Me Smile: F___It Thoughts:

- _____
- _____
- _____
- _____
- _____
- _____
- _____

_____

_____

_____

_____

Thoughts At F___It Forties

Thoughts That Make Me Smile: F__It Thoughts:

- _____

- _____

- _____

- _____

- _____

- _____

_____

_____

_____

_____

Thoughts At F___It Forties

Thoughts That Make Me Smile: F___It Thoughts:

- _____

- _____

- _____

- _____

- _____

- _____

- _____

_____

_____

_____

_____

Date: _____

Thoughts At F___It Forties

Thoughts That Make Me Smile: F__It Thoughts:

- _____

- _____

- _____

- _____

- _____

- _____

- _____

_____

_____

"Coming apart at the seam, one stitch at a time, does not mean it will all explode into tethers."

(Blog: Like A Bird On A Wire…So Are The Days Of Our Lives Author: Gilda Tavernese)

Thoughts At F___It Forties

Thoughts That Make Me Smile: F___It Thoughts:

- _____
- _____
- _____
- _____
- _____
- _____

_____

_____

_____

_____

Thoughts At F___It Forties

Thoughts That Make Me Smile: F___It Thoughts:

- _____
- _____
- _____
- _____
- _____
- _____
- _____

_____

_____

_____

_____

Thoughts At F___It Forties

Thoughts That Make Me Smile: F__It Thoughts:

- _____

- _____

- _____

- _____

- _____

- _____

- _____

_____

_____

_____

_____

Thoughts At F___It Forties

Thoughts That Make Me Smile: F___It Thoughts:

* _____

* _____

* _____

* _____

* _____

* _____

* _____

_____

_____

_____

_____

Thoughts At F___It Forties

Thoughts That Make Me Smile: F___It Thoughts:

- _____
- _____
- _____
- _____
- _____
- _____

_____

_____

_____

_____

Thoughts At F___It Forties

Thoughts That Make Me Smile: F__It Thoughts:

- _____
- _____
- _____
- _____
- _____
- _____
- _____

_____

_____

_____

_____

Thoughts At F___It Forties

Thoughts That Make Me Smile: F___It Thoughts:

- _____

- _____

- _____

- _____

- _____

- _____

- _____

_____

_____

_____

_____

Thoughts At F___It Forties

Thoughts That Make Me Smile: F__It Thoughts:

- _____

- _____

- _____

- _____

- _____

- _____

- _____

_____

_____

"As time skips past me, I hope to soon
answer the call from across the sea-
for now only in my dreams."

(Blog: Ancient Ancestral Connections
Author: Gilda Tavernese)

Thoughts At F___It Forties

Thoughts That Make Me Smile: F___It Thoughts:

- _____
- _____
- _____
- _____
- _____
- _____
- _____

_____

_____

_____

_____

Thoughts At F___It Forties

Thoughts That Make Me Smile:　　　F___It Thoughts:

- _____

- _____

- _____

- _____

- _____

- _____

- _____

_____

_____

_____

_____

Date: _____

Thoughts At F___It Forties

Thoughts That Make Me Smile: F__It Thoughts:

- _____
- _____
- _____
- _____
- _____
- _____
- _____

_____

_____

_____

_____

Thoughts At F___It Forties

Thoughts That Make Me Smile: F__It Thoughts:

- _____
- _____
- _____
- _____
- _____
- _____
- _____

_____

_____

_____

_____

Thoughts At F___It Forties

Thoughts That Make Me Smile: F__It Thoughts:

- _____
- _____
- _____
- _____
- _____
- _____
- _____

_____

_____

_____

_____

Thoughts At F___It Forties

Thoughts That Make Me Smile: F__It Thoughts:

- _____
- _____
- _____
- _____
- _____
- _____
- _____

_____

_____

_____

_____

Thoughts At F___It Forties

Thoughts That Make Me Smile: F___It Thoughts:

- _____
- _____
- _____
- _____
- _____
- _____
- _____

_____

_____

_____

_____

Thoughts At F___It Forties

Thoughts That Make Me Smile: F___It Thoughts:

- _____

- _____

- _____

- _____

- _____

- _____

- _____

_____

_____

"Sometimes what we might bet our lives on, what we know to our core to be true...sometimes isn't true at all."

*(Blog: Perception: Maybe It's Really Nothing
Author: Gilda Tavernese)*

Thoughts At F___It Forties

Thoughts That Make Me Smile: F__It Thoughts:

- _____
- _____
- _____
- _____
- _____
- _____
- _____

_____

_____

_____

_____

Thoughts At F___It Forties

Thoughts That Make Me Smile: F__It Thoughts:

- _____
- _____
- _____
- _____
- _____
- _____
- _____

_____

_____

_____

_____

Thoughts At F___It Forties

Thoughts That Make Me Smile: F___It Thoughts:

- _____

- _____

- _____

- _____

- _____

- _____

- _____

_____

_____

_____

_____

_____

Thoughts At F___It Forties

Thoughts That Make Me Smile: F__It Thoughts:

- _____
- _____
- _____
- _____
- _____
- _____
- _____

_____

_____

_____

_____

Thoughts At F___It Forties

Thoughts That Make Me Smile: **F___It Thoughts:**

- _____
- _____
- _____
- _____
- _____
- _____
- _____

_____

_____

_____

_____

Thoughts At F___It Forties

Thoughts That Make Me Smile: F___It Thoughts:

- _____

- _____

- _____

- _____

- _____

- _____

- _____

_____

_____

_____

_____

Thoughts At F___It Forties

Thoughts That Make Me Smile: **F___It Thoughts:**

- _____

- _____

- _____

- _____

- _____

- _____

- _____

_____

_____

_____

_____

_____

Thoughts At F___It Forties

Thoughts That Make Me Smile: **F___It Thoughts:**

- _____
- _____
- _____
- _____
- _____
- _____
- _____

_____

_____

"Language is important because it sets the tone for change."

(Blog: STRONZA!
Author: Gilda Tavernese)

Thoughts At F___It Forties

Thoughts That Make Me Smile: F__It Thoughts:

- _____
- _____
- _____
- _____
- _____
- _____
- _____

_____

_____

_____

_____

Thoughts At F___It Forties

Thoughts That Make Me Smile: F___It Thoughts:

- _____
- _____
- _____
- _____
- _____
- _____

_____

_____

_____

_____

Thoughts At F___It Forties

Thoughts That Make Me Smile: F___It Thoughts:

- _____
- _____
- _____
- _____
- _____
- _____

_____
_____
_____
_____

Thoughts At F___It Forties

Thoughts That Make Me Smile: F__It Thoughts:

- _____

- _____

- _____

- _____

- _____

- _____

- _____

_____

_____

_____

_____

_____

Thoughts At F___It Forties

Thoughts That Make Me Smile: F__It Thoughts:

- _____
- _____
- _____
- _____
- _____
- _____
- _____

_____

_____

_____

_____

Thoughts At F___It Forties

Thoughts That Make Me Smile: F__It Thoughts:

- _____

- _____

- _____

- _____

- _____

- _____

- _____

_____

_____

_____

_____

Thoughts At F___It Forties

Thoughts That Make Me Smile: F___It Thoughts:

- _____
- _____
- _____
- _____
- _____
- _____
- _____

_____

_____

_____

_____

Date: _____

Thoughts At F___It Forties

Thoughts That Make Me Smile: F__It Thoughts:

- _____

- _____

- _____

- _____

- _____

- _____

- _____

_____

_____

*"I am an instrumental influence,
but also just a simple instrument..."*

*(Blog: A Pathway Through Time
Author: Gilda Tavernese)*

Thoughts At F___It Forties

Thoughts That Make Me Smile: F__It Thoughts:

- _____
- _____
- _____
- _____
- _____
- _____
- _____

_____

_____

_____

_____

Thoughts At F___It Forties

Thoughts That Make Me Smile: F__It Thoughts:

- _____

- _____

- _____

- _____

- _____

- _____

- _____

_____

_____

_____

_____

Thoughts At F___It Forties

Thoughts That Make Me Smile: F___It Thoughts:

- _____

- _____

- _____

- _____

- _____

- _____

- _____

_____

_____

_____

_____

Thoughts At F___It Forties

Thoughts That Make Me Smile: F__It Thoughts:

- _____
- _____
- _____
- _____
- _____
- _____
- _____

_____

_____

_____

_____

Thoughts At F___It Forties

Thoughts That Make Me Smile: F___It Thoughts:

- _____
- _____
- _____
- _____
- _____
- _____
- _____

_____

_____

_____

_____

Thoughts At F___It Forties

Thoughts That Make Me Smile: F__It Thoughts:

- _____

- _____

- _____

- _____

- _____

- _____

_____

_____

_____

_____

Thoughts At F___It Forties

Thoughts That Make Me Smile: F___It Thoughts:

- _____
- _____
- _____
- _____
- _____
- _____
- _____

_____

_____

_____

_____

Date: _____

Thoughts At F___It Forties

Thoughts That Make Me Smile: F__It Thoughts:

- _____
- _____
- _____
- _____
- _____
- _____
- _____

_____

_____

"I want to hear about their accomplishments, but I'm certain I can learn more from their failures and faults..."

(Blog: After I Die Just Be Honest!
Author: Gilda Tavernese)

Date: _____

Thoughts At F___It Forties

Thoughts That Make Me Smile: F___It Thoughts:

- _____
- _____
- _____
- _____
- _____
- _____
- _____

_____

_____

_____

_____

Thoughts At F___It Forties

Thoughts That Make Me Smile: F__It Thoughts:

- _____
- _____
- _____
- _____
- _____
- _____
- _____

_____

_____

_____

_____

Thoughts At F___It Forties

Thoughts That Make Me Smile: F__It Thoughts:

- _____
- _____
- _____
- _____
- _____
- _____
- _____

_____

_____

_____

_____

Thoughts At F___It Forties

Thoughts That Make Me Smile: F__It Thoughts:

- _____
- _____
- _____
- _____
- _____
- _____
- _____

_____

_____

_____

_____

Thoughts At F___It Forties

Thoughts That Make Me Smile: **F___It Thoughts:**

- _____
- _____
- _____
- _____
- _____
- _____
- _____

_____

_____

_____

_____

Thoughts At F___It Forties

Thoughts That Make Me Smile: F__It Thoughts:

- _____
- _____
- _____
- _____
- _____
- _____
- _____

_____

_____

_____

_____

Thoughts At F___It Forties

Thoughts That Make Me Smile: F___It Thoughts:

- _____

- _____

- _____

- _____

- _____

- _____

- _____

_____

_____

_____

_____

_____

Thoughts At F___It Forties

Thoughts That Make Me Smile: **F___It Thoughts:**

- _____
- _____
- _____
- _____
- _____
- _____
- _____

*"I shall patiently await for my package
from Amazon, my crowning glory-
that feeling that I am deserving of
such a crown in motherhood."*

*(Blog: My Mother's Day Crown?
Waiting For Amazon To Deliver It Of Course!
Author: Gilda Tavernese)*

Thoughts At F___It Forties

Thoughts That Make Me Smile: F__It Thoughts:

- _____
- _____
- _____
- _____
- _____
- _____
- _____

_____

_____

_____

_____

Thoughts At F___It Forties

Thoughts That Make Me Smile: F___It Thoughts:

- _____

- _____

- _____

- _____

- _____

- _____

- _____

_____

_____

_____

_____

Thoughts At F___It Forties

Thoughts That Make Me Smile: F___It Thoughts:

- _____

- _____

- _____

- _____

- _____

- _____

- _____

_____

_____

_____

_____

Thoughts At F___It Forties

Thoughts That Make Me Smile: F__It Thoughts:

- _____
- _____
- _____
- _____
- _____
- _____
- _____

_____

_____

_____

_____

Thoughts At F___It Forties

Thoughts That Make Me Smile: F__It Thoughts:

- _____
- _____
- _____
- _____
- _____
- _____

_____

_____

_____

_____

Thoughts At F___It Forties

Thoughts That Make Me Smile: F__It Thoughts:

- _____
- _____
- _____
- _____
- _____
- _____

_____

_____

_____

_____

Thoughts At F___It Forties

Thoughts That Make Me Smile: **F__It Thoughts:**

- _____
- _____
- _____
- _____
- _____
- _____
- _____

_____

_____

_____

_____

Thoughts At F___It Forties

Thoughts That Make Me Smile: F___It Thoughts:

- _____

- _____

- _____

- _____

- _____

- _____

- _____

_____

_____

"Just a couple of strutting swans amongst ducks, but all I see are birds."

(Blog: Pride
Author: Gilda Tavernese)

Thoughts At F___It Forties

Thoughts That Make Me Smile: F__It Thoughts:

- _____
- _____
- _____
- _____
- _____
- _____
- _____

_____

_____

_____

_____

Thoughts At F___It Forties

Thoughts That Make Me Smile: F__It Thoughts:

- _____
- _____
- _____
- _____
- _____
- _____
- _____

_____

_____

_____

_____

Thoughts At F___It Forties

Thoughts That Make Me Smile: F___It Thoughts:

- _____
- _____
- _____
- _____
- _____
- _____
- _____

_____

_____

_____

_____

Date: _____

Thoughts At F___It Forties

Thoughts That Make Me Smile: F__It Thoughts:

- _____
- _____
- _____
- _____
- _____
- _____
- _____

_____

_____

_____

_____

Thoughts At F___It Forties

Thoughts That Make Me Smile: F__It Thoughts:

- _____

- _____

- _____

- _____

- _____

- _____

- _____

_____

_____

_____

_____

Date: _____

Thoughts At F___It Forties

Thoughts That Make Me Smile: F__It Thoughts:

- _____

- _____

- _____

- _____

- _____

- _____

- _____

_____

_____

_____

_____

Thoughts At F___It Forties

Thoughts That Make Me Smile: F__It Thoughts:

- _____
- _____
- _____
- _____
- _____
- _____
- _____

_____

_____

_____

_____

_____

Thoughts At F___It Forties

Thoughts That Make Me Smile: F___It Thoughts:

- _____

- _____

- _____

- _____

- _____

- _____

- _____

_____

_____

*"As parents, just because we can,
doesn't always mean we should."*

*(Blog: Parenting: The Moment You Take A Back Seat
Author: Gilda Tavernese)*

Thoughts At F___It Forties

Thoughts That Make Me Smile: F__It Thoughts:

- _____
- _____
- _____
- _____
- _____
- _____
- _____

_____

_____

_____

_____

Thoughts At F___It Forties

Thoughts That Make Me Smile: F__It Thoughts:

- _____
- _____
- _____
- _____
- _____
- _____
- _____

_____

_____

_____

_____

Date: _____

Thoughts At F___It Forties

Thoughts That Make Me Smile: F__It Thoughts:

- _____
- _____
- _____
- _____
- _____
- _____
- _____

_____
_____
_____
_____

181

Thoughts At F___It Forties

Thoughts That Make Me Smile: F__It Thoughts:

- _____
- _____
- _____
- _____
- _____
- _____
- _____

_____

_____

_____

_____

Date: _____

Thoughts At F___It Forties

Thoughts That Make Me Smile: F__It Thoughts:

- _____
- _____
- _____
- _____
- _____
- _____
- _____

_____

_____

_____

_____

Thoughts At F___It Forties

Thoughts That Make Me Smile: F__It Thoughts:

- _____
- _____
- _____
- _____
- _____
- _____
- _____

_____

_____

_____

_____

Thoughts At F___It Forties

Thoughts That Make Me Smile: F__It Thoughts:

- _____

- _____

- _____

- _____

- _____

- _____

- _____

_____

_____

_____

_____

Thoughts At F___It Forties

Thoughts That Make Me Smile: F___It Thoughts:

- _____
- _____
- _____
- _____
- _____
- _____
- _____

"Your 40s are a time to get to know yourself better, discover your true essence, what makes you unique."

(Blog: TAFF Club:
Bad Habits, Spoiled, Or Simply Set In Our Ways?
Author: Gilda Tavernese)

Thoughts At F___It Forties

Thoughts That Make Me Smile: F__It Thoughts:

- _____
- _____
- _____
- _____
- _____
- _____
- _____

_____

_____

_____

_____

Thoughts At F___It Forties

Thoughts That Make Me Smile: F___It Thoughts:

- _____

- _____

- _____

- _____

- _____

- _____

- _____

_____

_____

_____

_____

Thoughts At F__It Forties

Thoughts That Make Me Smile: F__It Thoughts:

- _____
- _____
- _____
- _____
- _____
- _____
- _____

_____

_____

_____

_____

Thoughts At F___It Forties

Thoughts That Make Me Smile: F___It Thoughts:

- _____
- _____
- _____
- _____
- _____
- _____
- _____

_____

_____

_____

_____

Thoughts At F___It Forties

Thoughts That Make Me Smile: F__It Thoughts:

- _____
- _____
- _____
- _____
- _____
- _____
- _____

_____

_____

_____

_____

Thoughts At F___It Forties

Thoughts That Make Me Smile: F__It Thoughts:

- _____
- _____
- _____
- _____
- _____
- _____
- _____

_____

_____

_____

_____

Thoughts At F___It Forties

Thoughts That Make Me Smile: F___It Thoughts:

- _____
- _____
- _____
- _____
- _____
- _____
- _____

_____

_____

_____

_____

Thoughts At F___It Forties

Thoughts That Make Me Smile: F___It Thoughts:

- _____
- _____
- _____
- _____
- _____
- _____
- _____
_____
_____

*"I probably don't say this enough,
but I like who I am today."*

*(Blog: "Don't Ever Change"
Author: Gilda Tavernese)*

Thoughts At F___It Forties

Thoughts That Make Me Smile: F___It Thoughts:

- _____
- _____
- _____
- _____
- _____
- _____
- _____

_____

_____

_____

_____

Date: _____

Thoughts At F___It Forties

Thoughts That Make Me Smile: F__It Thoughts:

- _____

- _____

- _____

- _____

- _____

- _____

- _____

_____

_____

_____

_____

Thoughts At F___It Forties

Thoughts That Make Me Smile: F__It Thoughts:

- _____
- _____
- _____
- _____
- _____
- _____
- _____

_____

_____

_____

_____

_____

Thoughts At F___It Forties

Thoughts That Make Me Smile: F__It Thoughts:

- _____

- _____

- _____

- _____

- _____

- _____

- _____

_____

_____

_____

_____

Thoughts At F___It Forties

Thoughts That Make Me Smile: F__It Thoughts:

- _____
- _____
- _____
- _____
- _____
- _____
- _____

_____

_____

_____

_____

Thoughts At F___It Forties

Thoughts That Make Me Smile: F__It Thoughts:

- _____
- _____
- _____
- _____
- _____
- _____
- _____

_____

_____

_____

_____

Thoughts At F___It Forties

Thoughts That Make Me Smile: F__It Thoughts:

- _____

- _____

- _____

- _____

- _____

- _____

- _____

_____

_____

_____

_____

Thoughts At F___It Forties

Thoughts That Make Me Smile: F___It Thoughts:

* _____

* _____

* _____

* _____

* _____

* _____

* _____

_____

_____

"Our heroes, whom we cheer on, all the
while were always there. Unsung."

(Blog: All The While. Unsung.
Author: Gilda Tavernese)

Date: _____

Thoughts At F___It Forties

Thoughts That Make Me Smile: F__It Thoughts:

- _____
- _____
- _____
- _____
- _____
- _____
- _____

_____

_____

_____

_____

Thoughts At F___It Forties

Thoughts That Make Me Smile: **F__It Thoughts:**

- _____
- _____
- _____
- _____
- _____
- _____
- _____

_____

_____

_____

_____

Thoughts At F___It Forties

Thoughts That Make Me Smile: F__It Thoughts:

- _____

- _____

- _____

- _____

- _____

- _____

- _____

_____

_____

_____

_____

_____

Thoughts At F___It Forties

Thoughts That Make Me Smile: F___It Thoughts:

- _____
- _____
- _____
- _____
- _____
- _____

_____

_____

_____

_____

Thoughts At F___It Forties

Thoughts That Make Me Smile: **F__It Thoughts:**

- _____
- _____
- _____
- _____
- _____
- _____
- _____

_____

_____

_____

_____

Thoughts At F___It Forties

Thoughts That Make Me Smile: F__It Thoughts:

- _____

- _____

- _____

- _____

- _____

- _____

- _____

_____

_____

_____

_____

Thoughts At F___It Forties

Thoughts That Make Me Smile: F___It Thoughts:

- _____

- _____

- _____

- _____

- _____

- _____

_____

_____

_____

_____

Date: _____

Thoughts At F___It Forties

Thoughts That Make Me Smile: F___It Thoughts:

- _____
- _____
- _____
- _____
- _____
- _____
- _____

_____

"I may never be a pretty princess in pink with a perfectly placed tiara, but I am the queen of my castle now, and that suits me just fine."

(Blog: Always The 'Old Lady',
Never the 'Young Princess'
Author: Gilda Tavernese)

Thoughts At F___It Forties

Thoughts That Make Me Smile: F___It Thoughts:

- _____
- _____
- _____
- _____
- _____
- _____
- _____

_____

_____

_____

_____

Thoughts At F___It Forties

Thoughts That Make Me Smile: F___It Thoughts:

- _____

- _____

- _____

- _____

- _____

- _____

- _____

_____

_____

_____

_____

Thoughts At F___It Forties

Thoughts That Make Me Smile: F___It Thoughts:

- _____
- _____
- _____
- _____
- _____
- _____
- _____

_____

_____

_____

_____

Thoughts At F___It Forties

Thoughts That Make Me Smile: F__It Thoughts:

- _____

- _____

- _____

- _____

- _____

- _____

- _____

_____

_____

_____

_____

Thoughts At F___It Forties

Thoughts That Make Me Smile: F___It Thoughts:

- _____

- _____

- _____

- _____

- _____

- _____

- _____

_____

_____

_____

_____

Thoughts At F___It Forties

Thoughts That Make Me Smile: F___It Thoughts:

- _____

- _____

- _____

- _____

- _____

- _____

- _____

_____

_____

_____

_____

_____

Date: _____

Thoughts At F___It Forties

Thoughts That Make Me Smile: F___It Thoughts:

- _____
- _____
- _____
- _____
- _____
- _____
- _____

_____

_____

_____

_____

217